WHAT'S THE ELECTORAL COLLEGE?

By Donna Reynolds

Published in 2025 by
KidHaven Publishing, an Imprint of Greenhaven Publishing, LLC
2544 Clinton Street
Buffalo, NY 14224

Designer: Deanna Lepovich
Editor: Jennifer Lombardo

Photo credits: Cover (top) vesperstock/Shutterstock.com; cover (bottom) Varga Jozsef Zoltan/Shutterstock.com; p. 5 Rob Crandall/Shutterstock.com; p. 7 mark reinstein/Shutterstock.com; p. 9 Pyty/Shutterstock.com; p. 11 Strawberry Blossom/Shutterstock.com; p. 13 brichuas/Shutterstock.com; p. 15 Courtesy of the Library of Congress; p. 17 Everett Collection/Shutterstock.com; p. 19 (top) THONGCHAI.S/Shutterstock.com; p. 19 (bottom) Mihai_Andritoiu/Shutterstock.com; p. 21 Asmar Bayram/Shutterstock.com.

Library of Congress Cataloging-in-Publication Data

Names: Reynolds, Donna, 1976- author.
Title: What's the electoral college? / Donna Reynolds.
Other titles: What is the electoral college?
Description: Buffalo, NY : KidHaven Publishing, [2025] | Series: What's the issue? | Includes index.
Identifiers: LCCN 2023057274 | ISBN 9781534547896 (library binding) | ISBN 9781534547889 (paperback) | ISBN 9781534547902 (ebook)
Subjects: LCSH: Electoral college–United States–Juvenile literature. | Elections–United States–Juvenile literature. | Voting–United States–Juvenile literature.
Classification: LCC JK529 .R48 2025 | DDC 324.6/3–dc23/eng/20231213
LC record available at https://lccn.loc.gov/2023057274

Printed in the United States of America

CPSIA compliance information: Batch #CSKH25: For further information contact Greenhaven Publishing LLC at 1-844-317-7404.

Please visit our website, www.greenhavenpublishing.com. For a free color catalog of all our high-quality books, call toll free 1-844-317-7404 or fax 1-844-317-7405.

CONTENTS

Not a Place

When you think of a college, you probably think of a big school. However, the Electoral College isn't a place. It's a group of people who are involved in presidential elections.

Every four years, the United States holds a presidential election. Voters go to their **polling place** and cast their vote for the person they want to win the election. The number of votes each **candidate** gets is called the popular vote. However, the popular vote isn't what decides who will be president—the Electoral College is. If you think this sounds confusing, you're not alone! Many people say this system is **complicated**.

Facing the Facts

The word "college" comes from the Latin word *collegium*, which means a group of people who work together. The Electoral College is a group of people who work together to elect a president.

Polling places are often set up in schools, community centers, and other public buildings.

Choosing the Electors

The United States has two main political parties—the Republican Party and the Democratic Party. A political party is a group of people who generally have the same beliefs about how a country's government should be run.

Each party holds national and state **conventions**. Most electors—the people who make up the Electoral College—are chosen at their state's convention. Some states have other ways of choosing electors. Often, being picked as an elector is a way for a party to **reward** members who have done a lot of good work for it.

Facing the Facts

Each political party has a color **associated** with it. The Democrats have blue, and the Republicans have red. When people talk about "blue states" and "red states," they mean states where more than half of the population voted for the candidate of a certain political party.

This picture shows the crowd at the 2016 Republican National Convention.

Winning the States

Each state has a certain number of electors. This number is the same as the number of senators and **representatives** each state has in Congress. The more populated a state is, the more electors it has. Most states have a "winner-takes-all" approach to electoral votes. In other words, when a candidate wins the popular vote in a state, they win all of that state's electoral votes.

The number of electors in the country always adds up to 538. Whichever candidate wins a majority, or more than half, wins the election. This means a candidate needs at least 270 electoral votes to become the president.

Facing the Facts

Washington, D.C., is not a state, but it has three electors.

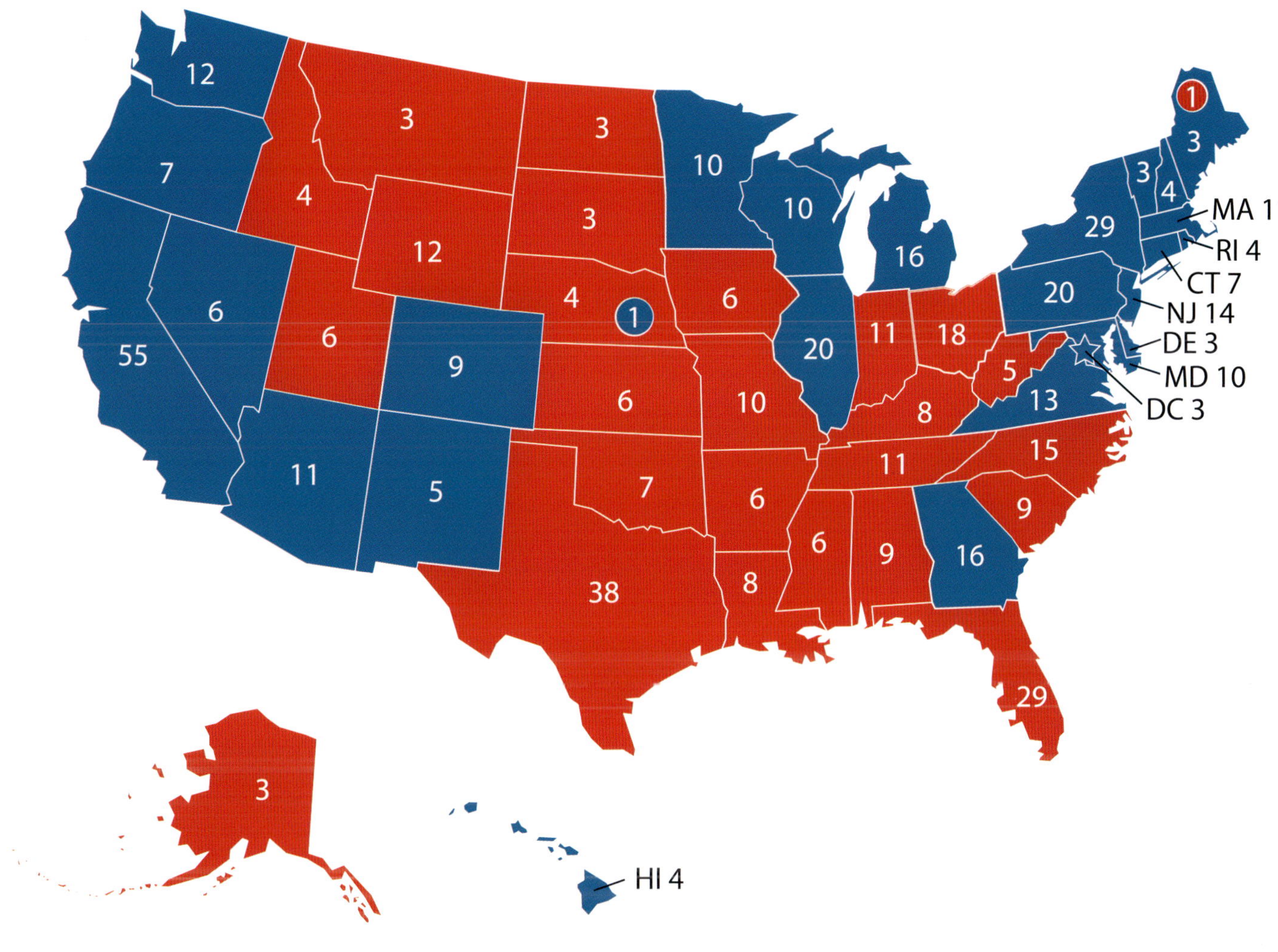

This map shows the Electoral College votes in the 2020 U.S. presidential election. Blue states cast votes for the Democratic candidate, Joe Biden. Red states cast votes for the Republican candidate, Donald Trump. Circles within a state show where electoral votes were divided, or split, between the two candidates, which can happen in some states.

A Closer Look

Let's look at Texas as an example of how the Electoral College works. Right now, Texas has 38 electoral votes. On Election Day, Texans go to their polling places to vote for president and vice president. Whoever gets the most votes in Texas wins all of Texas's electoral votes.

Election Day is held on the Tuesday after the first Monday in November. On the first Monday after the second Wednesday in December, 38 electors meet in Austin, the capital of Texas. Each casts one vote for president and one vote for vice president based on the popular vote.

Facing the Facts

Electoral votes are recorded on six copies of a **certificate**. Each copy includes the names of the people who received electoral votes for president and vice president in that state and the number of electoral votes they each received. All the electors sign the certificates.

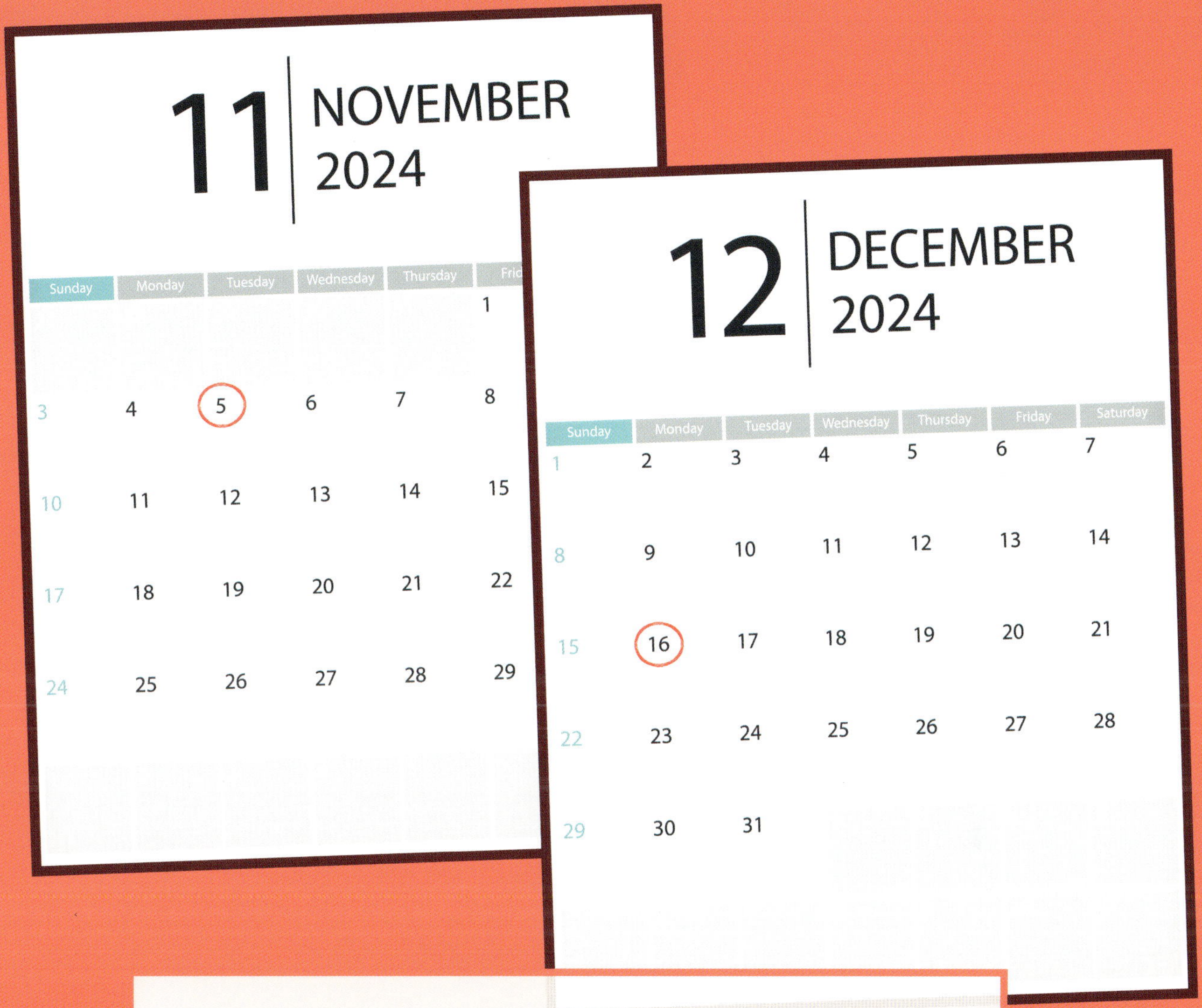

11 | NOVEMBER 2024

Sunday	Monday	Tuesday	Wednesday	Thursday	Frid
					1
3	4	5	6	7	8
10	11	12	13	14	15
17	18	19	20	21	22
24	25	26	27	28	29

12 | DECEMBER 2024

Sunday	Monday	Tuesday	Wednesday	Thursday	Friday	Saturday
1	2	3	4	5	6	7
8	9	10	11	12	13	14
15	16	17	18	19	20	21
22	23	24	25	26	27	28
29	30	31				

Before **digital** voting machines were invented, votes from all states had to be counted by hand. Then, the results had to be sent by mail. There's about a month between Election Day and when the Electoral College votes. In the past, people needed that time to get all of this done.

The District Method

Only two states—Maine and Nebraska—don't have a winner-takes-all approach. Instead, they split their electoral votes by congressional district. Most states have a large enough population to give them more than one representative in the House of Representatives. Those states are divided into areas called congressional districts, with one representative elected by each district.

In Maine and Nebraska during a presidential election, instead of winning the entire state at once, a candidate gets their electoral votes by winning the popular vote in each district. This is called the district **method**, or Maine-Nebraska method, of awarding electoral votes.

Nebraska has three congressional districts and five electors. This map shows that in 2020, Donald Trump won the popular vote in two of the districts (1 and 3), while Joe Biden won in the 2nd district. Biden got one electoral vote, and Trump got two. Trump also got the two electoral votes the state had left because he won the most popular votes in the state.

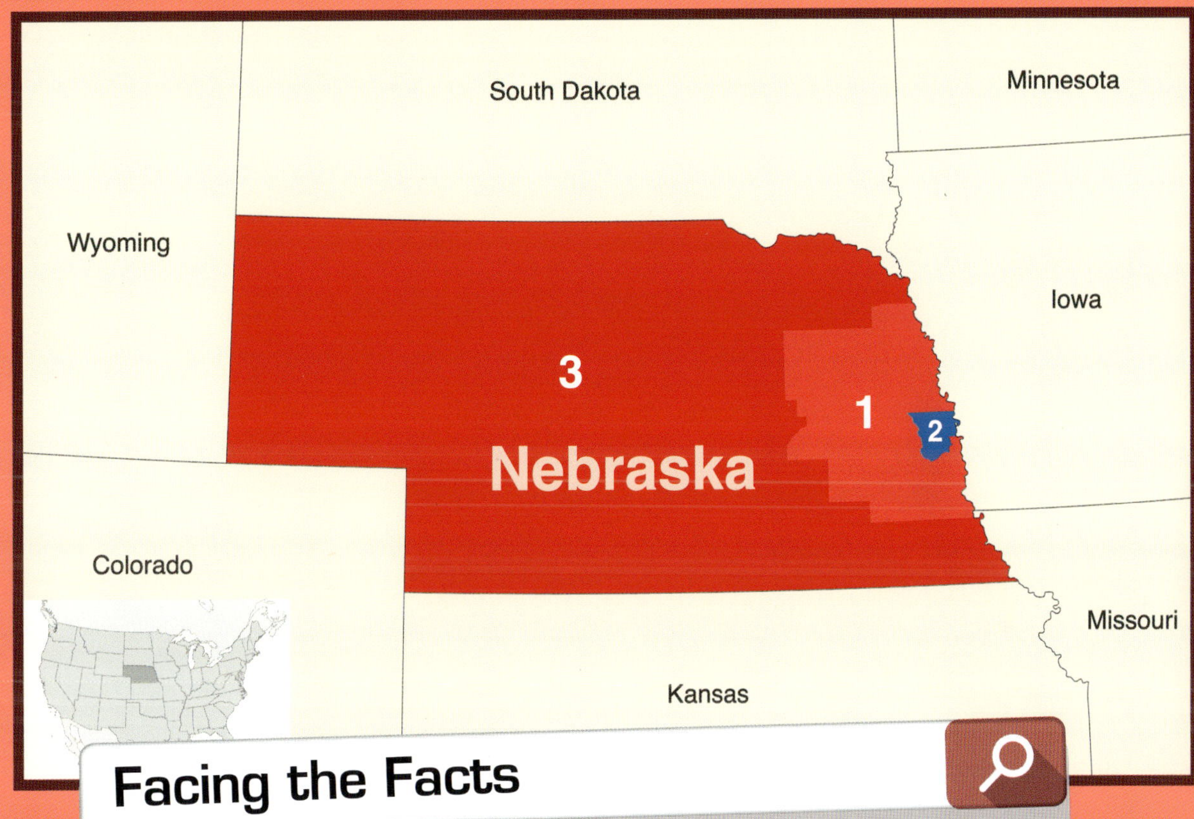

Facing the Facts

Maine started using the district method in 1972. Nebraska followed in 1992. Each state has had a split vote twice as of 2023. Nebraska was split in 2008, Maine was split in 2016, and both were split in 2020.

The Founding Fathers

Why do we elect our president this way? The answer goes back to when the United States first became a country. In 1787, the Founding Fathers met to talk about how the new country should work.

Some of the Founding Fathers thought the people should vote directly. In other words, they wanted to follow the popular vote. They were worried about giving the government too much power, like England's king had. Others thought Congress should choose the president. They believed most voters wouldn't know enough about the candidates to make a good choice. The Electoral College was a **compromise** between these two groups.

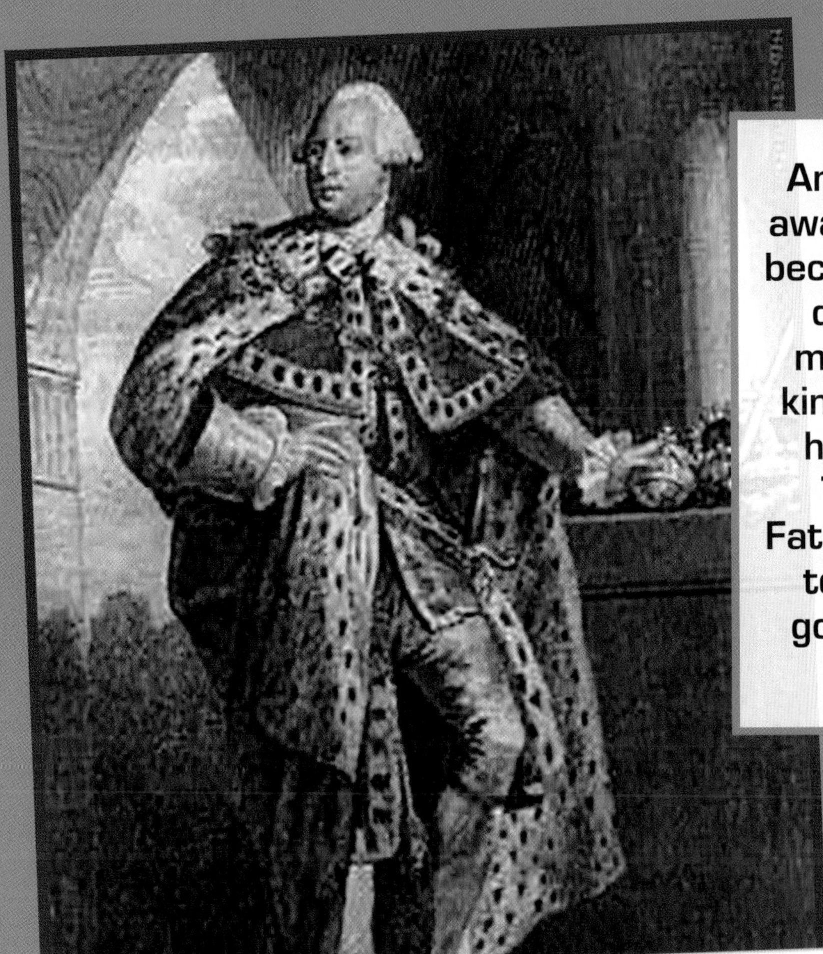

Americans broke away from England because Americans didn't like how much power the king (shown here) had over them. The Founding Fathers didn't want to give the new government that much power.

Facing the Facts

Putting the Electoral College in place meant that the electors would have the final say in who became president. The U.S. **Constitution** doesn't say electors have to follow their state's popular vote. Those who vote against the popular vote are often called "faithless electors."

Compromise

The Electoral College was a compromise in another way too. At the time, enslaved Black people made up a little more than one-third of the South's total population. However, they weren't allowed to vote. Southerners said a direct vote would be unfair. They wanted enslaved people to be counted toward their population. Northerners said it was unfair to count people who couldn't vote.

The Three-Fifths Compromise counted three-fifths of the enslaved population. The Electoral College combined direct voting (the popular vote) and indirect voting (the electors) so population would count for only part of the electoral **process**—the number of electoral votes from each state.

Facing the Facts

The Constitution says that if no presidential candidate gets a majority of the electoral votes, then the House of Representatives votes for the president. Each state gets one vote in this case.

Slavery played a large part in the Electoral College's formation. However, even after slavery was abolished, or done away with, the Electoral College stayed in place and worked the same way.

Is It Fair?

About 65 percent of Americans say the Electoral College is outdated, or too old to be useful anymore. The reasons it was created don't apply anymore. Voters today can use the internet to quickly learn all about the presidential candidates, and the 14th Amendment, or change, to the Constitution abolished the Three-Fifths Compromise.

Many people also say the Electoral College makes voting unfair. Studies have shown it gives more voting power to people in smaller states and swing states. Some states typically vote Republican, some typically vote Democrat, and others can "swing" either way. Those are the states candidates pay the most attention to.

Facing the Facts 

It's possible for a president to lose the popular vote but win the electoral vote. This has happened five times in U.S. history as of 2023.

Some people worry that without the Electoral College, people who live in large, very populated cities will have more voting power than people who live in small towns.

Getting Involved

The Electoral College can only be abolished by making an amendment to the Constitution. For this to happen, two-thirds of Congress needs to vote to pass the amendment. Then, three-fourths of the states need to ratify, or agree to, the amendment. That's not likely to happen.

Instead of completely abolishing the Electoral College, some people think we can change it to make it better. For example, Congress could pass a law saying that electors must follow their state's popular vote. You can help shape the American electoral process in years to come by learning more about the Electoral College and deciding where you stand.

Facing the Facts 

Congress has tried many times—more than 700 times, in fact—to change or abolish the Electoral College.

WHAT CAN YOU DO?

Use what you've learned to make your own decision about whether we should keep the Electoral College the way it is.

Learn more about how the Electoral College works.

Remind the adults in your life about the importance of voting, and go with them to vote.

Raise money for groups that fight for voting rights and help people register, or sign up, to vote.

Understanding how the Electoral College works is the first step toward forming your own opinions about it.

GLOSSARY

associated: Related, connected, or combined.

candidate: A person who runs in an election.

certificate: A document that is proof of some fact.

complicated: Difficult to understand or explain.

compromise: A way of settling an argument where each side gives up something they want.

constitution: The document that sets out the basic laws of a country.

convention: A meeting for a common purpose.

digital: Relating to electronics.

method: A way of doing something.

polling place: A place where people go to cast their vote in an election.

process: A series of actions leading to a result.

representative: A person who acts for a group of people.

reward: To give something nice to someone in exchange for a desirable action.

FOR MORE INFORMATION

WEBSITES

BrainPOP: Presidential Election

www.brainpop.com/socialstudies/usgovernment/presidentialelection

Watch a video, play games, and take quizzes to test your knowledge of how American presidential elections work.

270 to Win

www.270towin.com

This interactive website allows users to create their own projection of who will win upcoming elections.

BOOKS

Berne, Emma Carlson, Cari Meister, and Nel Yomtov. *The Kids' Complete Guide to Elections*. North Mankato, MN: Capstone Press, 2020.

Corso, Phil. *The Electoral College*. Buffalo, NY: PowerKids Press, 2020.

Shea, Therese. *What Is the Electoral College?* Buffalo, NY: Gareth Stevens Publishing, 2022.

INDEX